Nuts & Bolts

Writing Outstanding Journal Articles

Library of Congress Cataloging-in-Publication Data

Nuts and bolts : writing outstanding journal articles.
    p. cm.
    ISBN 978-1-937604-06-6
    Includes bibliographical references and index.
    1. Academic writing. 2. Scholarly publishing.
3. English language—Rhetoric. 4. Authorship.
I. American Association on Intellectual and
Developmental Disabilities.

PN146.N88 2012
808.02—dc23

                              2012031070

Printed in the United States of America

Table of Contents

Editor's Note

This book is the first of its kind to be published by AAIDD. It is hoped that writers across disciplines will find *Nuts & Bolts: Writing Outstanding Journal Articles* an excellent, easily accessible resource that offers guidance not only to authors, to help them get published, but also to professionals and students, to help them improve their general research, writing, and reporting skills.

Clearly, over the last two decades, much has changed in the world at large; in the world of scholarly publishing; and in the technologies that students, teachers, researchers, authors, editors, and publishers use on a daily basis. However, what remains constant, and confirms the necessity of this guide, is the fact that writing is a requisite proficiency, an essential skill for professional success—perhaps now, in an era of rapid communications and endless distractions, more than ever before. Hence, this new resource was born out of the knowledge that authors, even those firmly entrenched in the age of "content consumption," need references that will enable them to improve their writing and research skills and that will help to familiarize them with, and consequently engage them in, the publishing process of both print and electronic products.

This edition contains chapters dedicated to the "nuts and bolts" of writing for journals; the purpose, content, and structure of various article types; a section on style and mechanics for scholars; basic manuscript submission guidelines; and an examination and explanation of policies and issues involved in "fair use" and the public domain that will aid authors in determining when and if it is necessary to acquire permission for reuse of print and online material.

As I considered the contents and structure of this guide, my goal was not to reinvent the wheel—as there are other guides dedicated to writing for publication—but to build upon the extant literature and offer the most up-to-date information for authors seeking publication and for students, teachers, and other professionals needing guidance to help them improve their general writing and research skills. *Nuts & Bolts: Writing Outstanding Journal Articles* offers essential writing and research practices and standards: Readers will learn how to steer clear of common compositional pitfalls; to avoid the most frequently committed errors encountered by journal editors in the social sciences; to write concisely and in bias-free language; to cite and credit sources appropriately; and to create meaningful, well-constructed reference lists. Though AAIDD journals are used as examples of these traits, this edition provides information that can be applied to professional publications across many disciplines. The successful application of the standards exemplified in this book will facilitate the communication of ideas and research and simplify the tasks of students, authors, editors, publishers, and—most important—today's voracious "content consumers."

Lisa M. O'Hearn, MA
Director, Publications Program
AAIDD

Foreword

I t is one thing to know how to do research and an entirely different challenge to communicate the outcomes. No matter one's technical prowess in theory, design, and analysis, the writing of research will often seem an entirely unnatural act to the novice. A casual survey of resources on academic publishing finds endless advice on writing about research. Whereas the details of the messages vary, the core themes appear the same. There are broadly stated norms about academic expectations and vague admonitions that the good manuscript is equal parts (or some such ratio) inspiration and perspiration. Take the complex and communicate it simply. Be scholarly but not pretentiously so. Focus on the grand synthesis but obsessively attend to the minutiae of style. Describe all things relevant, except what is obvious, and do it in a handful of pages.

This is fine advice of course, but in the absence of a detailed road-map there is substantial room for error. For many years I have directed a seminar on dissertation writing and learned, to my chagrin, the capacity of graduate students to generate nearly endless variations of the bad research report. Although students present instructors with many fine teachable moments, punishing the bad and banal is not the most efficient path to good research writing.

One must begin with a framework—a scaffolding if you will, upon which the theoretical narrative, and reporting of methods, results and interpretations can be constructed. In AAIDD's *Nuts & Bolts: Writing Outstanding Journal Articles,* you will find the blueprint in the form of a user-friendly guide for planning and constructing a research paper: the elements of style, the organization of a research paper, the different writing objectives for the different forms of research reports, a demystification of the publishing process, and of course, instructions on the minutiae and mechanics of style. The ways of academic publishing can be arcane; this succinct update of writing and publication guidelines will reduce your quota of perspiration and, along the way, provide new insights on the process of communication through writing. Read and write. You need only add more inspiration.

—Glenn T. Fujiura
Editor-in-Chief,
Intellectual and Developmental Disabilities

Introduction
Nuts & Bolts: Writing Outstanding Journal Articles, At a Glance

The book is organized in three parts:

Part I: Articles and Approaches offers three essays offering descriptions of The Research Article, The Review Article, and The Theoretical Article and guidance on the writing and submission of these types of manuscripts.

Part II: Mechanics and Style addresses writing techniques; methods of data presentation; and the mechanics of grammar, spelling, punctuation, and usage. This section, which is a distillation of the AAIDD Publications Program internal style manual, is provided as an easy reference guide for authors. These chapters focus on correcting the most common errors AAIDD staff editors encounter in academic, scholarly, and professional writing.

Part III: Submission and Publication focuses on the scholarly peer-review system; provides basic instructions on how to submit journal manuscripts and book proposals; and sketches, briefly, typical publication production procedures, including brief chapters on copyright and permissions, "fair use," and the public domain.

Part I
Articles and Approaches

The Research Article

Publishing should be considered part and parcel of professional life for a researcher because the dissemination of results and findings is integral to the research process. Research in any field advances by means of testing the validity and exploring the implications of previous research. Although writing "scientifically" must be learned—as there are standard forms, lexicons, and styles that seasoned readers absolutely expect of the literature to which they choose to attend—doing so need not be a daunting process. This chapter aims to guide the researcher through the "ins and outs" of writing research articles that will be considered worthy of publication in scholarly and academic journals.

Whereas the content, style, and organization of a research article are vitally important, the process leading to publication is equally critical. Scientific articles of all types must be *valid;* that is, to have a discernible effect, they must be published in peer-reviewed journals in the respective field of study. When published in the "wrong" type of publication—for example, a trade or news magazine—even the most excellent research article will not be considered "validly published." For nearly three centuries of developing tradition, editorial practices, codes of ethics, and publication procedures, scholars have struggled with the definition of *valid publication.*

Valid Publication

Robert A. Day, who for many years was the vice president of the Institute for Scientific Information, one of the world's largest producers of information services covering the professional literature, defined a *scientific article* as a written published report describing original research results (Leithauser & Bell, 1987). Day qualified this short definition by indicating that a scientific article must be written in a certain standard style and format and must be published in a certain way. The Council of Biology Editors, an authoritative organization of scientific editors who frequently deal with such problems of definition, asserted that a valid primary scientific publication must comprise original research in a peer-reviewed journal that will enable peers to

- assess observations,
- repeat experiments, and
- test conclusions. (Derntl, 2003)

Organization

Thus, a research article is organized to meet the requirements of a valid publication. The article must be stylized per the conventions of its respective field, with distinct components. For example, the research article written for the social sciences/health and mental health genre should comprise at least, and in the following order, an Introduction, Method, Results, Discussion, and References section. For at least 50 years, the tendency toward this organizational, formal unity has been prescribed and accepted as a standard. Hence, the most well-written research articles report original data in this eminently logical fashion and in the conventional, agreed-upon lexicon of the particular field of study.

Title. Although the sections described in the previous paragraph form the basis of the research article, there are additional parts of an article that are also of importance, such as the title and the abstract.

The title of the article will be, undoubtedly, its most read part. The number of readers who will find an article relevant to their area of inquiry increases significantly the more accurate and concise the article title is. According to Day and Gastel (2006), a good title comprises the fewest possible words that adequately describe the contents of an article. Thus, effective titles

- identify the main problem investigated in the article;
- begin with the subject of the article;
- are accurate, unambiguous, specific, and complete;
- do not contain abbreviations (unless they are well-known by the target audience); and
- attract specific readers. (Peat, Elliott, Baur, & Keena, 2002, p. 94)

Abstract. A good abstract is a one-paragraph summary of the whole article. Abstracts have become increasingly important as electronic publication databases are currently the primary means by which scholars locate research reports in a given subject area. Only information relevant to potential readers should be included in the abstract.

Abstracts for research articles should describe, in as few sentences as possible,

- the problem under investigation;
- the participants/sample, specifying pertinent demographic characteristics;
- the salient features of the study methodology, including terms most likely to be used in electronic searches;
- the findings, including effect sizes and/or significance levels; and
- the conclusions or implications/applications. (American Psychological Association [APA], 2010, p. 26)

This type of abstract is called an *informative abstract* because it extracts everything relevant from the article, such as primary research objectives addressed, methods used to solve the identified problem, results obtained, and conclusions drawn. Such abstracts often serve as a highly aggregated substitute for the full-text article.

Following is a checklist indicating relevant parts of an abstract; each of these constituent parts should be packed into one sentence whenever possible:

- ► Why should readers care about the problem and the results?
- ► What problem is the article attempting to solve, and what is the scope of the work?
- ► What was done to explore the problem?
- ► What do the results indicate?
- ► What conclusions/implications do the results suggest?

Authors should note that some things do not belong in an abstract, such as information and conclusions not stated in the article, references to other literature, the exact title phrase, and references to illustrative elements such as tables and figures. It is also vital for authors to be aware that when preparing a research article for submission, they should take care to ensure that they do not exceed the word limit ascribed to abstracts for the journal in which they hope to publish. Typically, abstract word limits range from 150 to 250 words, but the strictures vary from journal to journal. The word limit and other submission guidelines can be found in the "Information for Authors" section of the journal, which is usually published in the print version and can be found, most commonly, on the publisher's Web site.

Introduction. The body of a research article should open with the presentation of the problem under examination and should describe, in brief, the study methodology. The best introductions answer the following questions in as few pages as possible and give the reader a firm understanding of what was done and why.

- ► Why is this research or the problem important?
- ► Has there been previous study of this problem? If so, and if that previous research was published, how does this article build on the earlier literature?

- ▶ What are the objectives of the present research?
- ▶ How do the objectives and research design correlate?
- ▶ What are the implications of this particular study?

Method. The Method section of a research article provides the methodology used in a study or experiment. Authors should provide detailed information on the research design, participants, equipment, materials, and conceptual and operational definitions of the variables used in the study. The Method section should provide enough information to allow other researchers to replicate the study, so inclusion of specific product names and model numbers for equipment/materials is usually appropriate.

Results. The Results section should be a summary of the analyses performed on the data collected. All relevant results should be mentioned—even those that run counter to expectations: Do not make the mistake of omitting results that are not aligned with the original hypothesis. Discussion of the results, whether or not they were expected, should be reserved for the Discussion section.

Discussion. The Discussion section should offer your evaluation and interpretation of the implications of the results, specifically with respect to the original hypothesis. This section should open with a clear statement and should acknowledge the limitations of the research, if any. In this section, the work of others can be used to confirm and contextualize your conclusions. If an intervention is presented in the article, indicate whether it was successful and why or why not. Discuss the characteristics that make the intervention applicable to circumstances beyond the scope of the study. The Discussion section should conclude with "a reasoned and justifiable commentary on the importance of your findings" (APA, 2010, p. 36). Finally, you might wish to recap the reasons that the problem under examination is important, what issues might pivot on the findings, and what suggestions are confirmed (or not) by the application of these findings to broader circumstances.

References. This section is a list of the work of previous scholars that was cited in text. There are two purposes for the reference list: to ensure that readers can place your work in the context of previous research and theory and so that readers can reliably locate the previous studies you have used to support the need for your research.

The list should be in alphabetical order, by first author's surname or by the full name of the authoring organization. The standard procedures for citation, as established by APA guidelines, ensure that references are accurate, complete, and useful to investigators and readers (APA, 2010, p. 37). For more exhaustive information on reference lists and in-text citations, see Section II: Mechanics and Style.

References

American Psychological Association. (2010). *Publication manual of the American Psychological Association* (6th ed.). Washington, DC: Author.

Day, R. A., & Gastel, B. (2006). *How to write and publish a scientific paper.* Westport, CT: Greenwood Press.

Derntl, M. (2003). *Basics of research paper writing and publishing.* Unpublished doctoral dissertation, University of Vienna, Vienna, Austria.

Leithauser, G. G., & Bell, M. P. (1987). *The world of science: An anthology for writers.* New York: Holt, Rinehart and Winston.

Peat, J., Elliott, E., Baur, L., & Keena, V. (2002). *Scientific writing: Easy when you know how.* London: BMJ Books.

The Review Article

Scientists and scholars commonly use review articles as a forum to communicate with one another and with the public. There is a wide range of review article styles (sometimes called *literature reviews*), ranging from those directed at disabilities professionals, psychologists, biologists, chemists—and the interdisciplinary list continues—to those aimed at a more general audience (e.g., reviews published in publications such as *Scientific American*).

The purpose of writing review articles is to sum up the current state of the research on a particular topic. However, the review article is not primarily a summary; rather, it comments on and evaluates the works under examination in the light of specific issues and theoretical concerns. Ideally, the writer presents all the relevant elements of his or her chosen topic, maps out the current range of positions—providing readers a coherent view of the current state of knowledge on the topic—then defines his or her own position in the remainder of the article.

The most effective review articles identify the following:

- ► the main researchers/practitioners writing/working in the field,
- ► recent major advances and discoveries,
- ► significant gaps in the research,
- ► current debates,
- ► implications of the findings, and
- ► where (and possibly how) further research should be conducted.

Thus, the good review article combines a summary of the articles under examination and critical comments centered on the findings or arguments posed in the articles; they should provide to the reader a place from which to mine the key articles for any given topic. If you write a good review article, and your audience thoroughly digests its contents, they should be able to "talk the talk" about the topic under discussion.

Unlike research articles, review articles are good places to get a basic idea about a topic. However, there is a "problem" aspect to review articles: They can sometimes contain mind-numbing banks of citations and can resemble a protracted contact list—tons of names and numbers, but no substance. Thus, before you write your review, ask yourself whether it is likely to be interesting to your intended audience. If the answer is "no," you can do one of two things: scrap the idea or make it interesting, perhaps by extending its reach or setting it in a broader context. As an antidote to the dullness that can plague review articles, authors should "take risks in choosing topics, writing articles, and making submissions" and not be deterred because "they represent too much of a departure from current conventions, whether in conceptualization or methodology" (Sternberg, 1991, p. 3).

Regardless of the topic, the ability to read and comment critically and clearly on a number of articles, without putting the readers to sleep, is the most important skill the author of review articles can develop. The beauty of this type of expository writing is that there are many organizing strategies that can be effectively used—that is, there is no one right way to write a review. A coherent review emerges from a clear conceptual structuring of the domain being reviewed—and if the review is organized by relationship rather than by chronology, then you are likely on your way to writing a good one (Bem, 1995). With that said, it is often helpful to give readers an overview of your review's structure and content; but beyond that, avoid commenting on your own writing. "Expository prose fails its mission if it diverts the reader's attention to itself and away from the topic; the process of writing should be invisible to the reader" (Bem, 1995, p. 172).

Good writers, regardless of genre, are necessarily focused on their readers, putting the interests of their audience first. Unfortunately, the topics, the writing styles, the tones and word choices in the numerous manuscripts AAIDD staff editors read convince us, unequivocally, that many writers do not recognize this necessity—instead, they aim to impress an imagined editor-in-chief or panel of reviewers, which is the most common and serious mistake a writer can make. Experienced editors and reviewers have already positioned themselves as the intended audience; like savvy gold miners, they deftly discern the real thing from pyrite, discarding the latter without hesitation. Thus, an author's separation from his or her intended audience will more often than not result in outright rejection of a manuscript. Conversely, those writers whose manuscripts are published will have consciously aligned themselves with their readers—that is, they will have taken the time and made the effort to know their audience.

Only after an author knows the target audience can the writing process begin. Firmly grasping the desires and knowledge levels of that particular audience enables an author to determine how much information to include, how subjective or objective the "voice" should be, and how formal or informal the prose—in short, how best to write.

Part and parcel of knowing various reading constituencies, and thus responding to their wants and needs, is researching and selecting appropriate publishing houses or journals to which to submit manuscripts. Writers who have done their homework and who have sought out presses that speak to their target audience—and, most important, who have read a vast amount in their genre—are the ones who are most likely to get published. The reading component of such preliminary research in particular is what enables writers to develop manuscripts that sound, look, and feel like publishable review articles. Essentially, reading is to writing as sowing is to reaping; many novice writers are like gardeners attempting to coax crops from soil that has not been properly tilled. If an aspiring writer has read few journal articles, he or she is unlikely to write one worth publishing. This is the absolute meaning of the well-known adage, "Write what you know."

Once you have finished writing a review that captures all of the elements of your topic and exposes them and explores them in the ways depicted in this chapter, do not make the most common mistake novice authors commit regularly: Do not submit the draft—and, yes, at this stage it is just a draft—until you have gone through the process of rewriting. For many writers, regardless of level of experience, revising a manuscript can be an agonizing process. Thus, because we are hardwired to avoid pain, some writers among us skip this crucial step. So thrilled to just finish the manuscript, they think "Whew, I'm finished! What a relief!" Well, I'm here to tell you that if you have not edited, proofed, and sometimes even repeated those processes, you are not done. Do not make the mistake of thinking that you can clean up the loose ends after the article has been accepted for publication. Alas, if you fall prey to that erroneous idea, the day of publication will never arrive. Journal editors will not do the work for you: That is, they will not bother to try to seek out your genius—your brilliance must be clear. To increase the chances of writing a manuscript that will be accepted, you must not give short shrift to any part of the process.

Write. Revise. Polish. Proof. Submit.

References

Bem, D.J. (1995). Writing a review article for *Psychological Bulletin. Psychological Bulletin, 118,* 172–177.

Sternberg, R.J. (1991). Editorial. *Psychological Bulletin, 109,* 3–4.

The Theoretical Article

Theoretical articles are basically "essays," containing or referring to a set of new or established abstract principles related to a specific field of knowledge. They should present an argument that is not essentially based on practical research. Characteristically, they do not contain original empirical or experimental data. The purpose of a theoretical article is for the author to draw on existing research to advance theoretical work in the field of interest; these articles can report on all aspects of the subject, including psychological, sociological, and ethical concerns.

The development of theory is traced to expand and refine theoretical constructs. Often the author will present a new theory of his or her own, indicating how the new theory links with previous theories and literature. Alternately, the author may analyze existing theories to highlight flaws and internal inconsistencies; or the author may focus on the advantages or superiority of one theory over another. Authors often bolster their arguments by examining a theory's internal consistency, external validity, and empirical support.

A good theoretical article includes the following:

- ► a thorough discussion of how the theory or model under review works,
- ► the principle upon which the theory or model is based,
- ► what the theory or model accounts for, and
- ► its associations to empirical results.

Theoretical Framework

A theoretical framework consists of concepts, their definitions, and existing theories that you will use for your particular study. The theoretical framework must demonstrate an understanding of the theories and concepts that are relevant to the topic of your manuscript and that will relate it to the extant literature and the broader field.

A theoretical framework is not something that is found readily available in the literature. You must review pertinent research literature for theories and analytic models that are relevant to the research problem you are investigating. The selection of a theory should depend on its appropriateness, ease of application, and explanatory power.

A solid theoretical framework serves to strengthen the manuscript in the following ways:

- ▸ An explicit statement of theoretical assumptions permits the reader to evaluate them critically.
- ▸ The theoretical framework connects the researcher to existing knowledge. Guided by a relevant theory, you are given a basis for your hypotheses and choice of research methods.
- ▸ Articulating the theoretical assumptions of a research study forces you to address questions of why and how. It permits you to move from simply describing an observed phenomenon to generalizing about various aspects of that phenomenon.
- ▸ Having a theory helps you to identify the limits to those generalizations. A theoretical framework specifies which key variables influence the phenomenon of interest. It alerts you to examine how those key variables might differ and under what circumstances.

By virtue of its applicatory nature, good theory in the social sciences is of value precisely because it fulfills one primary purpose: to explain the meaning, nature, and challenges of a phenomenon or various phenomena, often experienced but unexplained, so that practitioners and policymakers, among others, might use the knowledge to resolve problems in more informed, effective, and evidence-based ways.

Strategies for Developing the Theoretical Framework

A theoretical framework is used to limit the scope of the relevant data by focusing on explicit variables and defining the particular viewpoint that you will take in analyzing and interpreting the data, understanding the concepts and variables according to the given definitions, and building the knowledge base by validating or challenging theoretical assumptions.

The following are some strategies that will aid in the development of an effective theoretical framework:

- State your research problem. The problem anchors your entire study and forms the basis from which you must construct your theoretical framework.
- Clearly and concisely define the key variables in your research. Group these variables into independent and dependent categories.
- Answer the following question: What factors contribute to the presumed effect?
- Review the key theories related to the problem and choose the theory or theories that can best explain the relationships between the key variables you have identified.
- Discuss the assumptions or propositions of the theory or theories of choice and discuss how they are relevant to the present research.

Theories are the conceptual basis for understanding, analyzing, and designing ways to investigate relationships within social systems. Thus, in addition to the strategies delineated in the preceding paragraph, do the following to further flesh out your theoretical frame:

- discuss how important issues are identified,
- pose the critical research questions that need to be answered to maximize understanding of the problem,

- report the strategies used by the authors to indicate which data among the accumulated knowledge are relevant/important and which are not,
- identify the means by which data can be interpreted and coded for future use,
- explore how aging data are given new interpretations and new meaning,
- analyze new responses to problems that have no previously identified solutions, and
- explain how to guide and inform future research so that it can be applied to improve professional practice.

Characteristics of Published Theoretical Articles

In terms of AAIDD journals, and most other journals in the social sciences, a theoretical article (sometimes referred to as a *conceptual article*) typically describes an innovative approach to education, supports, intervention, policymaking, or a learning issue relevant to the respective field of inquiry. Theoretical articles published by AAIDD are strongly grounded in the relevant theoretical literature in functional areas such as education, supports, adaptive behavior, or psychology, and in the literature specific to the innovative approach or issue being described. The focus may be on a single approach or issue or on a comparison and contrasting of alternative approaches or issues. Because their purpose is to lay the foundation for future research in the field or area of study, publishable theoretical articles develop a set of propositions about the effectiveness of the approach or issue. What is most important to AAIDD editors and peer reviewers is that theoretical articles focus on cutting-edge topics and present significant new insights.

Part II
Mechanics and Style

Bias-free Writing

In the interest of accurate and unbiased communication and AAIDD's commitment to the fair and equitable treatment of individuals and groups, language in AAIDD publications may not imply ethnic, racial, sexual, or other kinds of discrimination, stereotyping, or bias.

These guidelines are intended to provide assistance to authors to help them portray people as accurately and as vividly as possible, eliminate bias from their writing, honor the richness of intellectual and cultural diversity, and use language that is accessible and inviting to readers.

The categories that follow are arranged alphabetically.

Disability

Do not refer to people with disabilities *as* their disabilities. For example, do not use the term "epileptics;" instead identify these individuals as "people with epilepsy."

Gender

Sex refers to biological differences: chromosomes, hormonal profiles, internal and external sex organs. *Gender* describes the characteristics that a society or culture delineates as masculine or feminine. Your writing should honor this distinction.

Recast writing that uses male or female pronouns to include all people. Use plurals when possible to avoid gender reference.

Ensure that terms for groups of men and women are parallel. Do not use the terms *male* and *female* as nouns; use as adjectives only.

Change terms that give the impression that only people of one gender perform certain duties or work in certain professions.

Use specific sexual identities instead of collecting different groups under a general heading.

HIV/AIDS

Avoid language that may imply a moral judgment on behavior or lifestyles. Prefer "people with AIDS" not "AIDS victims." Prefer "high-risk behavior" over "high-risk groups," which suggests that demographic traits may be responsible for AIDS exposure.

Race and Ethnicity

All languages evolve over time, incorporating new terms that better describe people. Ascertain the most acceptable current terms through Internet and/or library research and use the contemporarily acceptable terms consistently. Be mindful not to use two or more separate, yet acceptable terms interchangeably.

As often happens, people within certain groups disagree on preferred terms, thus AAIDD does not object to using alternate terms, such as Black and African American, within one article or chapter, as long as the context is clear, consistent, and will not cause confusion.

Whenever possible, use specific racial and ethnic identities instead of collecting different groups under a general heading.

Describe people in terms of what they are, instead of what they are not. For example, edit away from the terms *nonwhite* or *nonparticipant.*

Abstract and Key Words

A journal abstract should be between 150 and 250 words and should indicate both the purpose of the article and the conclusions reached. Abstracts should be written using specific, concrete language. Steer away from data, jargon, clichés, slang, and reference citations. Change "this paper" or "this manuscript" to "this article/book" or "the present article/book."

Each regular journal article (excluding columns) should include up to five key words, listed in alphabetical order, that describe the topic and population under discussion. After writing the manuscript, consider how well the key words reflect the content. Remember that these terms will be used for codification by abstracting services and electronic databases, so terms should have as few words as possible. In general, avoid the use of adjectives—change them to noun forms.

Example:

Vaccine-Related Beliefs and Practices of Parents of Children with Autism Spectrum Disorders

Abstract

Although the assertion of a link between vaccines and autism has been scientifically rejected, the theory continues to be popular and may influence the attitudes of parents of children with autism spectrum disorders. The authors sought to assess how often parents change or discontinue their child's vaccine schedule after autism spectrum disorder diagnosis and whether beliefs about the etiology of autism affect their decision to do so. The authors surveyed 197 (43%) of 460 eligible parents of children under 18 years of age with autism spectrum disorders who were enrolled in a state-funded agency that provides services to those with developmental disabilities in western Los Angeles County. Half of parents discontinued or changed vaccination practices, and this was associated with a belief that vaccines contributed to autism spectrum disorders, indicating a potential subset of under-vaccinated children. Educational tools should be designed to assist physicians when talking to parents of children with autism spectrum disorders about vaccination.

Key Words: autism; vaccines; autism spectrum disorders; parental beliefs

# Capitalization

Academic Degrees

Capitalize abbreviations of degrees, eliminating periods. Lowercase degrees when spelled out.

> Examples:
> MA
> PhD
> master of arts
> master's degree
> doctoral degree

Following a Colon

A complete sentence following a colon begins with a capital letter. A horizontal and vertical list following a colon begins with a lowercase letter, except when items in a vertical list are complete sentences. In those instances capitalize the first word of each item and end it with a period.

> Examples:
> 1. He asserted the following: Most states will opt for administrative review panels.
> 2. The following symptoms must be present in the patient:
>   ► mild fever or chills
>   ► sore throat
>   ► painful lymph nodes

Following an Em Dash (—)

In the title and in the references section of an article, the first letter of the first word following an em dash is capitalized.

Items in a Series

Do not capitalize nouns followed by numerals or letters that denote a specific place in a numbered series.

> Examples:
> chapter 4
> page 6
> day 1
> experiment 3

> Exceptions:
> The following are specific exceptions to this rule: Table 1, Figure 2, Type I or Type II errors, Axis V

Organizations

Lowercase all shortened or substitute names of councils, committees, commissions, chapters, et cetera. Official names of such (that is, when they are used as proper nouns) should be capitalized.

Prepositions

Capitalize all prepositions in the names of organizations if that is how the group identifies itself.

> Example:
> Mothers Against Drunk Driving

Tests, Scales, Models, and Forms

Capitalize the proper name of any form, checklist, scale, subscale, index, and so forth that the author uses and cites in an article. There should be an author–date citation after its first mention.

Lowercase the names of models.

Time

A.M. and P.M. should be set in small caps with periods, closed up.

Titles and Headings

Capitalize all words in (and figure and table) titles, except for prepositions, conjunctions, articles, and "to" in infinitives. Also, capitalize the first word after a colon or em dash. When a capitalized word is hyphenated, capitalize the second and subsequent parts of the compound, except for articles, prepositions, and coordinating conjunctions.

Unit modifiers are capitalized as if they were separate words, and words with a hyphenated prefix are not capitalized unless the word is a proper noun or proper adjective.

Examples:
Up-to-date information
Follow-Up Data
Self-esteem Measure
Strategies for Re-establishment

Figures and Tables. Capitalize main words in table column headings; capitalize only the first word in table stub columns. Capitalize in-text references to specific figures and tables but do not capitalize in-text references to equations, time periods, or units.

Job Titles and Offices. Lowercase all job titles, civic titles and offices, military titles and offices, religious titles and offices, and titles of nobility when they follow a name or are used in place of a name. Capitalize titles only when they precede the holder's name.

Figures

Separate figures from text and create a new Word document for each.

Ensure that all figures are numbered consecutively (beginning with Figure 1) and that all figures are called out in text.

Ensure that data given in text matches that displayed in figures. Text should explain, not simply repeat, data displayed in figures.

Authors must provide written permission from the original copyright holder if figures are adapted or are to be reprinted. If you are unsure as to the originality of a figure, query the author to confirm that the figure is original to the article and to publication. Authors are responsible for any fees involved in obtaining permission for reprinting. Source lines for figures must contain complete publication information for the original figure, including the page number. When the permission letter from the original copyright holder specifies language, that language should be reproduced exactly.

Captions

Edit figure captions for sense, length, and accuracy of information. Captions should enable figures to stand apart from text. Any information that is not needed in the caption should be deleted. Information that applies to the entire figure should be given in the notes to the figure; no superscripts should be used in figure captions.

Body

Edit figure text for style, clarity, and consistency.

Axes

Both horizontal and vertical axes should be labeled. Edit for caps, lowercase, bold, and centered. The vertical axis should be set vertically, running up the page.

Notes

Use the following formatting and order of elements:

> *Note.* Prose sentence. Acronym = definition; Acronym = definition; NA = not applicable (be sure to indicate, via a prose sentence, that "dashes" indicate that data are unavailable).
>
> *Source.* (or *Sources.*) [Specify Reprinted or Adapted] with permission (if not in the public domain) from [complete reference information in APA style, including specific page number, then permission wording specified in the permission letter, if applicable].
> [a]specific note.
> [b]specific note.
> [c]specific note.
> $^*p < .05.$ $^{**}p < .01.$ $^{***}p < .001.$

Italics

Use italics sparingly in text.

In Text

Italicize terms when first introduced only when the definition immediately precedes or follows the term. (Use quotation marks for words set apart as words that are not defined.)

Example:
During the 1860s, the psychiatric disorder *neurasthenia,* a neurosis characterized by weakness and fatigue, existed. In the 20th century, neurasthenia symptoms include. . .

The term "case management" has been used to refer to many different types of activity.

Legal Cases

Example:
The *Roe v. Wade* decision helped to. . .

Published Works

Titles of books, plays, motion pictures, essays, symphonies, operas, poems, pamphlets, newspapers, periodicals, and journals should be italicized. Italicize the name of a city in a newspaper title only when it is a specific part of the title. Give the city in parentheses after the name of the paper if it is not part of the proper name and the name is a common one.

> Examples:
> *New York Times*
> *Sun* (Baltimore), not *Baltimore Sun*

In Equations

All letters in equations (except Greek letters).

In References

Titles of books, plays, motion pictures, essays, symphonies, operas, poems, pamphlets, newspapers, periodicals, and journals should be italicized.

Italicize volume numbers that are part of a title or that indicate the volume number of a periodical.

In Tables

Italicize letters used as statistical abbreviations in table column headings and stubs.

Do Not Italicize . . .

- foreign words and abbreviations appearing in *Webster's Collegiate Dictioinary* (11th ed.), except *sic*
- slang words: Use quotation marks rather than italics for slang words at their first appearance only, if it is necessary to use slang at all.
- titles of unpublished matter, parts of published works (including chapters and journal articles), book series, radio and television programs, and short musical compositions. Instead, these elements should be set roman and within quotation marks.
- abstracting and indexing services, such as DIALOG and PsycINFO

Numbers

In general, spell out numbers one through nine and use figures for numbers 10 and above. However, always use numbers with million, billion, percent, and section and page numbers.

Examples:
three years, 10 years old, nine-year-old child, age 17, two weeks, one hour, 3 million, 11 billion, 1 percent, section 5, part 2, chapter 3, pp. 815

Use numbers when referring to specific points on a scale.

Examples:
rank subjects from 1 = *never* to 5 = *always*
but
a seven-point scale, a 10-point scale

Use numbers when referring to centuries or decades.

Examples:
During the 1960s (not during the sixties), 20th century

Use numbers to designate parts of books, experiments, and so forth.

Examples:
chapter 4, page 6, day 1, subject 3

Spell out ordinals up to, but not including, 10.

> Examples:
> fifth grade
> *but*
> grade 5
> third week
> *but*
> week 3
> 21st century, 10th conference

Spell out and hyphenate fractions that are less than one. Use figures with quantities that comprise whole numbers and fractions.

> Examples:
> two-thirds consensus
> one-half
> *but*
> 4½

Spell out numbers that begin a sentence (or rework the sentence).

> Example:
> Forty-five students responded. (A total of 45 students responded.)

With number ranges, use "to" in text. Use an en dash in tables and in the reference list.

> Example:
> The mortality rate of babies weighing 1,000 to 1,500 grams dropped from 50 percent in the late 1960s to 20 percent in the mid-1980s.

Mixing categories within a sentence is acceptable.

Example:
Three boys, ages four, five, and 11 years, and 14 teachers
participated in the study.

Spell out ages if referring to them generally.

Example:
Most of the respondents were in their forties.

Insert commas as appropriate in figures of 1,000 or more. Avoid
roman numerals, except with Type I or Type II errors and Axes I
through V of the *DSM*. (See also Statistics and Math section.)

Publishers

The following is a list of frequently cited publishers.

A

AAIDD, Washington, DC
Abingdon Press, Nashville, TN
Academic Press, San Diego
Addison-Wesley Press, Reading, MA
Aldine, New York
Aldine de Gruyter, New York
George Allen & Unwin, London
Allyn & Bacon, Boston
American Psychiatric Press, Washington, DC
American Psychological Press, Washington, DC
American Public Health Association, Washington, DC
American Public Welfare Association, Washington, DC
Appleton & Lange, Stamford, CT, or East Norwalk, CT
Jason Aronson, New York or Northvale, NJ
Aspen Publishers, Gaithersburg, MD
Athenuem, New York
Avon Books, New York

B

Ballantine Books, New York
Ballinger, Cambridge, MA, or New York
Bantam Books, New York

Basic Books, New York
Beacon Press, Boston
Behavioral Publications, New York
Bobbs-Merrill, Indianapolis or New York
Boston College, Chestnut Hill, MA
R. R. Bowker, New York or New Providence, NJ
Brandeis University Press, Waltham, MA
George Braziller, New York
Paul H. Brookes, Baltimore
Brookings Institution, Washington, DC
Brooks/Cole, Belmont, CA
Brown University Press, Providence, RI
Brunner/Mazel, New York

C

Cambridge University Press, Cambridge, England, or New York
The Catholic University of American Press, Washington, DC
Child Welfare League of America, Washington, DC
Columbia University Press, New York
Cornell University Press, Ithaca, NY
Council on Social Work Education, Alexandria, VA (1990 to
    present), New York (1989 and earlier)
Crown Books, New York

D

F. A. Davis, Philadelphia
Doubleday, Garden City, NY
Duke University Press, Durham, NC
E. P. Dutton, New York

E

Wm. B. Eerdmans, Grand Rapids, MI
Elsevier, New York
Elsevier Science, New York or Amsterdam
Lawrence Erlbaum, Hillsdale, NJ

F

Faber & Faber, London
Farrar, Straus & Giroux, New York
Fawcett Books, New York
Feminist Press, Old Westbury, NY
Follett, Chicago
Free Press, New York

G

Garland, New York
Greenwood Press, Westport, CT
Grosset & Dunlap, New York
Grove Press, New York
Grune & Stratton, New York or Philadelphia
Guilford Press, New York
Gulf Publishing, Houston

H

G. K. Hall, Boston or Thorndike, ME
Harcourt Brace Jovanovich, San Diego
Harper & Row, New York
HarperCollins, New York or London
Harrington Park Press, Binghamton, NY
Haworth Press, New York or Binghamton, NY
Heath, Lexington, MA
Heinemann, London
Hemisphere, New York or Washington, DC
Holt, Rinehart & Winston, New York
Horizon Press, New York or Tucson, AZ
Houghton Mifflin, Boston
Human Sciences Press, New York
Humanities Press, Atlantic Highlands, NJ

I

Indiana University Press, Bloomington
International Universities Press, New York or Madison, CT
Iowa State University Press, Ames
Richard D. Irwin, Homewood or Burr Ridge, IL

J

Jai Press, Greenwich, CT
Johns Hopkins University Press, Baltimore
Jossey-Bass, San Francisco

K

Alfred A. Knopf, New York

L

Lexington Books, Lexington, MA
J. B. Lippincott, Philadelphia
Little, Brown, Boston
Longman, New York or White Plains, NY
Louisiana State University Press, Baton Rouge

M

MIT Press, Cambridge, MA
McGraw-Hill, New York
Macmillan, New York or London
Charles E. Merrill, Columbus, OH
Methuen, London
Wm. Morrow, New York
C. V. Mosby, St. Louis
Mosby-Year Book, St. Louis

N

NASW Press, Washington, DC (1992 to present); Silver Spring, MD (1990 to 1991) (before 1990 the publisher was the National Association of Social Workers)

National Academies Press, Washington, DC (before 2000, publisher was National Academy)

National Association of Social Workers, Washington, DC (1992 to present); Silver Spring, MD (1983 to 1991); Washington, DC (1973 to 1982); New York (1972 and earlier)

National Education Association, Washington, DC

National Institutes of Health, Bethesda, MD

National Institute of Mental Health, Bethesda, MD

National Institute on Drug Abuse, Rockville, MD

New Directions, New York

New York University Press, New York

W. W. Norton, New York

O

Ohio State University Press, Columbus

Oxford University Press, New York or London

P

Pantheon Books, New York

E. Peacock, Itasca, IL

Penguin Books, New York

Pennsylvania State University Press, University Park

Pergamon Press, New York

Plenum Press, New York

Praeger, Westport, CT

Prentice Hall, Englewood Cliffs, NJ

Princeton University Press, Princeton, NJ

P. Putnam's Sons, New York

R

Rand McNally, Skokie, IL
Random House, New York
Rockefeller Institute of Government, Albany, NY
Routledge, London
Routledge, Kegan Paul, London or New York
Russell Sage Foundation, New York
Rutgers University Press, New Brunswick, *NJ*

S

Sage Publications, Thousand Oaks, CA (1994 to present);
    Newbury Park, CA (1987 to 1993); Beverly Hills, CA
    (1986 and earlier)
W. B. Saunders, Philadelphia
Schenkman Books, Rochester, NY
Schocken Books, New York
Scott, Foresman, Glenview, IL
Charles Scribner's Sons, New York
Simon & Schuster, New York
Southern Illinois University Press, Carbondale
Springer, New York
Springer-Verlag, New York
Stanford University Press, Stanford, CA
State University of New York Press (or SUNY Press), Albany
St. Martin's Press, New York
Syracuse University Press, Syracuse, NY

T

Tavistock, London
Temple University Press, Philadelphia
Charles C Thomas, Springfield, IL

U

UMI *See* University Microfilm International.

U.S. Department of Health and Human Services, Washington, DC (since May 1980)

U.S. Department of Health, Education, and Welfare, Washington, DC (before May 1980)

U.S. Government Printing Office, Washington, DC

University Microfilm International, Ann Arbor, MI (before 1996); UMI after January 1996)

University of Alabama Press, Tuscaloosa

University of Alaska Press, Fairbanks

University of Arizona Press, Tucson

University of Arkansas, Fayetteville

University of California Press, Berkeley or Los Angeles

University of Chicago Press, Chicago

University of Georgia Press, Athens

University of Hawaii Press, Honolulu

University of Idaho Press, Moscow

University of Illinois Press, Champaign

University of Iowa Press, Iowa City

University of Massachusetts Press, Amherst

University of Michigan Press, Ann Arbor

University of Minnesota Press, Minneapolis

University of Missouri Press, Columbia

University of Nebraska Press, Lincoln

University of New Mexico Press, Albuquerque

University of North Carolina Press, Chapel Hill

University of Oklahoma Press, Norman

University of Pennsylvania, Philadelphia

University of Pittsburgh Press, Pittsburgh

University of Puerto Rico Press, Rio Piedras

University of Southern California Press, Los Angeles

University of Tennessee Press, Knoxville
University of Texas Press, Austin
University of Toronto Press, Toronto
University of Utah Press, Salt Lake City
University of Washington Press, Seattle
University of Wisconsin Press, Madison
University Park Press, Baltimore
University Press of America, Lanham, MD
University Press of New England, Hanover, NH
Urban Institute, Washington, DC
Urban Institute Press, Washington, DC

V

Vanderbilt University Press, Nashville, TN
Van Nostrand Reinhold, New York
Viking Press, New York

W

Wadsworth, Belmont, CA
Warner Books, New York
Wayne State University Press, Detroit
Wesleyan University Press, Middletown, CT, or Hanover, NH
Westminster Press, Louisville, KY
Westview Press, Boulder, CO
Wiley/Blackwell, New York
John Wiley & Sons, New York
Williams & Wilkins, Baltimore

Y

Yale University Press, New Haven, CT

Punctuation

Ampersand

Use an ampersand or "and" in publisher names, according to publisher preference. Ensure that "&" versus "and" is consistent in journal titles in reference lists when a journal is cited more than once.

When a multiple-author reference in text is surrounded by parentheses, use an ampersand before the final author's name. If the reference is not enclosed in parentheses, then use "and." In the reference list, use the ampersand before the final author's name.

Apostrophe

Possessives of singular nouns take 's.

> Examples:
> Marx's theory
> Haynes's study

Possessives of most plural nouns take only an apostrophe.

> Examples:
> special educators' practices
> *but*
> children's
> women's

Use an apostrophe in expressions of duration.

Examples:

an hour's delay

20 years' experience

Do not use an apostrophe to form plurals of acronyms or numerals.

Examples:

PhDs

1920s

Brackets

Use brackets within parentheses for additional parenthetical material.

Example:

(Centers for Disease Control and Prevention [CDC], 1995)

However, parentheses are used within brackets in mathematical expressions.

Example:

$[F(2, 28) = 8.09, p < .001]$

Brackets should enclose interpolations in a quotation (see Quotations section).

When references fall within parenthetical statements, do not place the year of publication within brackets (see References section).

Colon

Use a colon after a grammatically complete sentence to introduce something that follows, such as a question, quotation, or list of examples. Following a colon, begin a complete sentence with a capital letter but begin items in a list with lowercase letters.

For vertical lists, use a colon after an introductory statement that constitutes a grammatically complete sentence. A colon does not precede a list of items that complete the introductory statement. (See examples under "Lists".)

Comma

Use commas to separate items in a series of three or more elements.

Use a comma before the conjunction.

Use commas to set off the elements in addresses and names of geographic places or political divisions.

Use a comma before and after the year when the exact day is included in the date. However, when only the month and year are included in the date, do not use commas to set off the elements.

Use commas to set off a nonessential or nonrestrictive clause; this is a clause that the sentence can do without.

> Example:
> These characteristics, which may vary, were common
>   among children with autism.

Do not use commas to set off an essential or restrictive clause, that is, a clause that identifies, limits, or defines the word it modifies.

Use a comma to separate two independent clauses joined by a conjunction.

> Example:
> Many parents were concerned about vaccines, but they
>   were unable to state which one in particular had
>   contributed to ASD.

Do not use a comma to separate compound predicates (two or more verbs having the same subject).

Use a comma before "but" in "not only . . ., but also" sentences.

Use a comma preceding Jr. and Sr., but not III and so on, unless that person prefers to leave it out.

Em Dash

Use an em dash to set off an abrupt thought or a change in the construction of a sentence.

En Dash

In heads and titles in all caps, use en dashes instead of hyphens wherever they occur.

Use an en dash with number ranges in tables, figures, page numbers, and references. In text, use "to" for ranges.

> Example:
> *American Journal on Intellectual and Developmental*
>   *Disabilities, 38,* 81–89
> *but*
> The women in the group were ages 25 to 40.

Use an en dash with the following compounds:
- ► a compound adjective in which one or both elements consist of two (nonhyphenated) words
- ► a compound adjective consisting or two nouns or adjectives of equal weight
- ► a prefix attached to an open compound adjective. (NOTE: Use a hyphen to attach a prefix to a hyphenated compound adjective.)
- ► a prefix attached to a compound noun

Hyphen

Place a hyphen between words combined to form a unit modifier immediately before the word modified, except in special cases.

Examples:
family-focused strategies
neighborhood-based approach
open-ended care
long-term-care referral

In cases in which the meaning is clear and readability is not improved, it is unnecessary to use a hyphen to form a temporary compound.

Examples:
civil rights legislation
high school student

In general, do not hyphenate unit modifiers used after the word modified.

Example:
He is not well known in this community, but he is a well-known man elsewhere.

Compounds with well-, ill-, better-, best-, little-, lesser-, and least- are hyphenated before the noun unless the compound carries a modifier.

Examples:
better-known clients
lesser-known clients

Hyphenate cardinal numbers plus unit measurements.

Examples:
15-minute meeting
three-month study

Hyphenate adjectival and noun compounds expressing fractions.

Examples:
one-half as much
two-thirds
7-month delay

Hyphenate when two or more compound words have a common base.

Examples:
fourth- and fifth-grade students
two-, three-, and four-year studies

Do not hyphenate compounds with the suffix "-like," unless they are formed with proper nouns, words ending with two "el"s, and word combinations.

Examples:
childlike
Chicago-like
bull-like

Do not hyphenate words denoting divisions or geographic or political areas that end with the suffix "-wide."

Examples:
communitywide
statewide
hospitalwide
worldwide
universitywide

Do not hyphenate a compound adjective that includes an adverb ending in "-ly."

Do not hyphenate compounds containing a Latin word.

Examples:
per copy rate
4 percent increase

Use a hyphen to attach a prefix to a proper noun or numeral.

Hyphenate words in which the meaning would be changed if the hyphen were not included.

Examples:
re-cover (to cover again)
re-formation (rather than reformation)

Use a hyphen to attach a prefix to a hyphenated compound adjective.

Example:
non-Spanish-speaking populations

Use a hyphen between the prefix and the base word when the last vowel of the prefix is the same as the first letter of the base word, but note exceptions in *Webster's*.

Examples:
re-establish
pre-existing
anti-intellectual
but
reenact
reinforce
reentry

Hyphenate when two or more prefixed words have a common base.

Example:
pre- and posttest

Items in a list should be parallel in construction.

Do not punctuate after items in a vertical list if those items are incomplete sentences or phrases. If items are phrases, then do not capitalize the first letter in each item.

The number of items in a numbered list must be specified in the sentence that introduces the list. If no number is mentioned, the list that follows should be a bullet list. Note that Arabic numerals rather than letters are used in numbered lists.

In vertical lists, if items are complete sentences, always capitalize the first word of each item. End each item with a period.

In some cases, lists contain both phrases and complete sentences. If some or all list items contain a complete sentence, end all items with a period.

Use parentheses around the numbers when a numbered list is incorporated into a sentence.

> Example:
> Four themes affected the women's assimilation into
>   the dominant social structure: (1) family needs,
>   (2) English-speaking ability, (3) the women's roles,
>   and (4) the schools' roles.

However, do not use parentheses in a vertical numbered list.

> Example:
> The group's three goals are to
>   1. educate group members about common problems, and
>   2. enhance group members' understanding of their
>   feelings improve communications.

Use separate sets of parentheses for different types of information.

> Examples:
> ($p = .03$) (Table 1)
> American Association on Intellectual and Developmental
>   Disabilities (AAIDD) (Smith & Wehmeyer, 2012)

Period

Do not use a period with acronyms or with academic degrees.

Examples:
AAIDD
AUCD
PhD
MA
but
U.S. (Use abbreviation only as an adjective; spell out
United States when used as a noun.)
P.L.

Do not use periods with initials or clients represented in case examples.

Quotation Marks

Use quotation marks to enclose the first occurrence of a term to indicate special meaning, slang, or irony. Do not use quotation marks for subsequent occurrences.

Use quotation marks to set off a word being used as a word. (But when the word is being defined, use italics.)

Example:
Consensus must be reached on how to define "village."

In addition, use quotation marks to enclose article or chapter titles mentioned in text.

Use single quotation marks to enclose a quote within a quote.

Example:
Weick and Pope (1988) reminded us that "only one person can truly 'know best,' and he or she is the person whose life is being lived" (p. 16).

Commas and periods go inside quotation marks; semicolons and colons go outside. Question marks and exclamation points go inside the quotation marks if they are part of the quotation; if not, they go outside.

Do not use quotation marks with words or phrases preceded by "so-called." (Refer also to Quotations section.)

Semicolon

In general, use a semicolon to separate items within a series with internal commas. Commas used in dates or to set off thousand digits or dependent clauses are not considered internal commas. However, when there are no commas within an item in the series, use commas to separate the elements.

Slash

AAIDD tries to avoid the use of slashes; they should be removed whenever possible. Sometimes a slash can be changed to an en dash; sometimes "and" or "or" should be used.

Edit "and/or" to be either "and" for inclusive statements or "or" for optional statements, or "or both" when optional and inclusive statements are implied.

Quotations

All quotations must be attributed to their original source, and the page number from the original source must be specified.

Permissions

Authors must obtain written permission from the copyright holder to use quotations from prose sources of more than 500 words. Authors are responsible for ensuring that quotations correspond exactly to the original wording, spelling (although typos can be fixed), and punctuation.

In addition, always query authors to confirm that tables and figures are original to the article and publication. If not, the author must provide written permission from the copyright holder to adapt or reprint.

Journal authors are responsible for any fees involved for reproducing tables or figures. (AAIDD pays permission fees for illustrations in AAIDD books.) Source lines must contain complete publication information for the original table or figure in reference style.

In cases in which a granted permission specifies wording, the wording should be reproduced exactly as requested.

Short Quotes

Place all quotes with fewer than 40 words within quotation marks.

Quotes that are within quotes should be enclosed within single quotation marks.

Cite the specific page number of the quote from the original source in parentheses after the close quote but before the period. However, do not cite a page number for quotes of five words or fewer.

Proverbial, biblical, and well-known literary expressions need not be set within quotation marks.

Delete quotation marks from around the words "yes" and "no," except in direct discourse.

Long Quotes

When a quotation is 40 words or more, the editor should indicate to the typesetter that it is to be set as an extract, and the typesetter will set according to style. Delete quotation marks from around extracts. Quotes that occur within the extract should be enclosed in double quotation marks.

When a paragraph break occurs in an extract, there should be no space between paragraphs, and the new paragraph should be indented.

A simple rule can be used to determine what punctuation precedes long quotes: A colon should be used only if the sentence preceding the quote is complete. If the sentence is incomplete, punctuate as would be grammatically correct if the quote were straight text.

Multiple Quotes

When an article contains many quotes (for example, from interview), all quotes regardless of length, may be set as extracts. When the quotes follow one another, they should be separated by three asterisks centered in the column.

Epigraphs

Epigraphs are set indented in italic without quotation marks. The author's full name and year of publication go on a separate line in roman, preceded by an em dash and flush right. A reference citation is not strictly necessary, but enough information should be given to give the reader a context for the quote (for example, the title or profession of the author, the date of the quote).

Changes in Quoted Material

Use three dots to indicate that words have been left out of the middle of a sentence in a quotation and four dots (a period and the three ellipses) to indicate that words have been omitted between sentences or after a sentence. If an entire paragraph (or line of poetry) has been left out, center five dots on a separate line.

The first letter of the first word of a quote may be changed to uppercase or lowercase without enclosing the letter in brackets. Delete ellipses at the beginning or end of an incomplete sentence.

If the author interpolates a word or phrase into a quotation, that word or phrase should be enclosed in brackets, not parentheses. If a quote in a manuscript contains parentheses, query the author to confirm that the parentheses are in the original.

When words not italicized in the original are italicized for emphasis, the notation "[italics added]" follows the quote and precedes the page number.

References

Any reference to earlier research, conceptual work, and so forth should be accompanied by a reference citation in text and complete reference information on the reference list. Similarly, all statistical data that are not part of primary research discussed in the article must be accompanied by a reference to the source of those data.

In rare cases, an author over-documents. It is not necessary to provide a reference citation for statements of well-known or historical facts, and it is not desirable to provide unwieldy lists of references. Unless the author's purpose is to be exhaustive, delete all but the most essential of the supporting references.

Reference citations in text or reference lists must be clear and complete.

AAIDD uses the author–date citation style set forth by American Psychological Association (see *Publication Manual of the American Psychological Association,* 6th ed., 2010).

Ways to Enhance Accuracy

Cross-reference all sources cited in text with entries on the reference list and verify that the spelling of author names and the dates are consistent. Ensure that all references on the list are cited in text.

If you change information in a reference, be sure to correct all citations of that reference throughout the article. In addition, ensure that the reference list is still in alphabetical order.

As you review a reference list, check to be sure that information that should be consistent throughout the list is so. For example, journal titles should be treated consistently, volume numbers for the same journal should correspond appropriately with the years, author's names should be spelled consistently, and so forth. Likewise, sometimes an author uses the same page numbers for two articles in the same issue of a journal.

In-Text Author–Date Citations

Parenthetical Citations. Arrange multiple author–date citations alphabetically by surname of the first author, then chronologically for sources by the same author. Order citations containing "et al." alphabetically in text, regardless of order in the reference list. Use a semicolon to separate reference citations within parentheses.

Use the past tense with in-text reference citations.

In a reference that appears in parenthetical text, use commas (not brackets) to set off the date.

Citations with Same Surname. If two references have the same author surname, include author initials in all text citations (regardless of year of publication).

    Example:

    (M. Henderson, 1990; V. Henderson, 1990)

Citation of Secondary Sources. Secondary citations (for example, "Jones, as cited in Roberts, 1990") are acceptable only if the primary source is unavailable. Only the secondary source should be listed on the reference list.

Personal Communications. Personal communications consist of letters, telephone conversations, interviews, and the like. Because they are not recoverable, personal communications are not included on the reference list. Use the following style in text: (personal communication with [first initial and last name], [title], [affiliation], [city and state abbreviation, if necessary], [month, day, and year of communication]).

Example:

(personal communication with R. Fischer, professor of
   social work, University of California, Los Angeles,
   May 20, 1992)

Alternatively, the name, title, and affiliation can go outside the parentheses and the words "personal communication" and the date inside.

Examples:

J. T. Jones, professor of sociology at the University of
   Maryland at College Park (personal communication,
   June 11, 1991), suggested. . .

B. R. Robinson, director of communications at Duvall Cor-
   poration in Dubuque, Iowa (personal communication,
   April 24, 1990), observed. . .

Nonparenthetical Citations. Once a reference has been cited in a paragraph, omit the year in subsequent nonparenthetical citations in that paragraph, unless the reference could be confused with others cited in the article (for example, when there are two references by the same author).

Example:

(See Table 2 of Philips & Ross, 1983, for complete data.)

Reference List

Check to be sure that entries are listed in alphabetical order (by surname of first author), then chronologically (earliest publication date first).

- ► Insert spaces between two initials; three initials should be bunched.

- ► Capitalize first word after colons and em dashes.
- ► Delete commas in page numbers.
- ► Delete "The" in titles of newspapers and periodicals in the reference list.

Examples:
Atlantic Monthly
Gerontologist
Nation
New Republic
New York Times
Sun

Citation Forms. Copy editors should check to ensure that the years for AAIDD journals correspond with the volume numbers.

Delete issue numbers from publications if you are certain that pagination is consecutive for the entire volume. The issue number *is* necessary when each issue of the periodical begins on page 1. If in doubt, leave the issue number. If the issue number is given for one citation from a journal, all other citations of that journal in the reference list must provide the issue number.

Legal References

Follow *The Blue Book: A Uniform System of Citation* (18th ed.) (familiarly called the "Blue Book") for citation forms of legal references. Note that court cases are italic in text and roman in the reference list.

Cite the name and year of an act in the text, along with the public law (P.L.) number. If possible, cite acts to the current official statute (according to the *United States Code Annotated,* Popular Name Table); otherwise, cite the official session laws.

Cities and States in Reference Citations

In reference citations and in text, the AAIDD follows Associated Press style for the omission of states and countries, except for Washington, DC. Use DC with Washington in text and in references.

Use the standard two-letter postal abbreviation for all states when listed in the reference list or the author blurb. In text, however, spell out the state name and include a comma before and after.

Do not cite the state with the following cities:

Atlanta	Honolulu	Oklahoma City
Baltimore	Houston	Philadelphia
Boston	Indianapolis	Pittsburgh
Chicago	Los Angeles	St. Louis
Cincinnati	Miami	Salt Lake City
Cleveland	Milwaukee	San Diego
Dallas	Minneapolis	San Francisco
Denver	New Orleans	Seattle
Detroit	New York	

Do not cite the country with the following cities:

Amsterdam	Luxembourg	Quebec
Beijing	Madrid	Rome
Berlin	Milan	Singapore
Copenhagen	Monaco	Stockholm
Geneva	Montreal	Tokyo
Havana	Moscow	Toronto
Hong Kong	Ottawa	Vatican City
Jerusalem	Paris	Vienna
London		

If the name of a state or country is in the name of an institution in a reference list, do not include the state or country with the city.

Example:

Tempe: Arizona State University.

Statistics and Math

The accuracy and appropriateness of the use of statistical measures are the responsibility of the author and manuscript reviewers. The editor who encounters statistical material must ensure that the material is formatted according to AAIDD style, using the *Publication Manual of the American Psychological Association* (6th ed.) as a guide. Whenever data in tables are discussed in the text, check to see that any numbers reported in the text (such as *n* values) agree with those in the tables. Also, for simple statistics, such as percentages, means, sample sizes, and *p* values, the editor should confirm the accuracy.

Reporting Requirements for Specific Tests

When the results of a statistical test are reported, certain elements of the test are essential to indicate to readers the importance of the results. A list of common statistical tests follows. Listed with each test are the elements that should be reported. If this material is not presented when the respective test is used, then the editor will query the author to provide it.

Analysis of Variance (ANOVA)

Report two degrees of freedom (*df*) values in parentheses and the probability (*p*) level. When reported parenthetically, enclose in brackets.

Examples:

$F(1, 28) = 15.75, p < .05$ or $[F(1, 28) = 15.75, p < .05]$

Chi Square

Report the degrees of freedom and the sample size in parentheses and the *p* value. When reported parenthetically, enclose in brackets.

Example:

$\chi^2(2, N = 100) = 5.61, p < .01$ or $[\chi^2(2, N = 100) = 5.62, p < .01]$

t tests

Report the *t* value, the degree of freedom, and the probability level or alpha level, as appropriate.

Example:

$t(2) = 1.16, p < .05$ or $[t(2) = 1.16, p < .05]$

Regression

Report the correlation coefficient (*r*) and probability level.

Example:

$(r = .86, p < .001)$

Computer Programs

If a statistical test is performed with a published computer program or a commercially available statistics package, name the test and cite the reference or the user's manual as appropriate. Do not cite the original reference for the statistical test.

For example, in text, with a procedure performed with SPSS software, name the procedure and cite the SPSS software or the names of the creator of the software, whichever is appropriate. Reference the manual for the software or the software itself in the reference list.

Examples:

SPSS, Inc. (1986). *SPSS use's guide.* New York: McGraw-Hill.

Jöreskog, K. G., & Sörbom, D. (1981). LISREL V: Analysis of linear structural equation modeling by maximum likelihood and least squares method. Uppsala, Sweden: University of Uppsala.

Common Statistical Abbreviations

df	degree of freedom
F	Fisher's F ratio
n	the number in a subsample
N	the number in the sample
p	probability level
r	Pearson product-moment correlation coefficient
r^2	coefficient of determination
R^2	coefficient of multiple correlations
SD	standard deviation
SE	standard error
t	the value of a t test
M	mean
χ^2	chi square
α	alpha
β	beta
σ	sigma
ANOVA	analysis of variance. Write it out at first mention.
MANOVA	multivariate analysis of variance. Write it out at first mention.

Math and Statistics Text Style

Decimal Fractions. Decimal fractions that are being compared and are all of the same measure should be consistently carried out to the same number of digits. (This rule also applies to tables.) For chi-square values, decimals are carried out to two places only.

In scientific contexts decimal fractions of less than 1.00 are set with an initial zero if the quantity expressed can exceed 1.00.

Examples:
$M = 0.73$, the ratio 0.85

If the quantity never reaches more than 1.00, as in probabilities, levels of significance, correlation coefficients, and factor loadings, no leading zero is used.

Examples:
$p = .05, r = .10$

Equations

In equations, italicize all letters (except Greek letters), unless directed otherwise by the author. Do not insert any punctuation after equations.

If an equation runs over one line, break before an operational sign.

Greek Letters

Spell out Greek letters in text. Use actual Greek letters only in equations and tables. Do not italicize Greek letters. Mark for the typesetter whether the letter is uppercase or lowercase.

NA, Em Dash

Query the meaning of an em dash or NA in tables when not specified. The em dash should indicate that data are not available, and NA should indicate "not applicable."

NS

Not significant is abbreviated NS (no italics). Use only in tables. Define in a note to the table.

Percent Symbol

Use a percent symbol only when preceded by a numeral and in tables. When discussing a range of percentages, repeat the symbol.

> Example:
> 15% to 30%

Use the word *percentage* when a number is not given.

Percentages, Numerals, and Sample Sizes (N and n values)

When authors report percentages, the N values (total sample size) and the n values (subsample size) must either be obvious given the data provided or specified in parentheses after the percentage (if the percentage is approximate—for example, "nearly one-third"—query for exact percentage). If one N or n value applies to a whole paragraph, the sample can be specified at the beginning of the paragraph and no parenthetical sample sizes are needed. Also, if percentages are listed in a table with their respective sample sizes, then none need be specified in the text.

Probability Levels

In tables, standard probability levels are denoted by asterisks. One asterisk is assigned to the highest p value, two asterisks to the next highest, and so on:

> *$p < .05$. **$p < .01$. ***$p < .001$.

Within an article, all tables that have a probability note should have the same number of asterisks assigned to the same values. Only the p values used in each table should be listed in the notes.

Scales

Scales are often used in generalizability studies involving Cronbach's alphas.

Edit toward the following construction:

... a three-point scale in which 1 = *never,* 2 = *sometimes,* and 3 = *often*

... a five-point scale ranging from 1 = *strongly agree* to 5 = *strongly disagree*

Query author for scale anchors if they are not provided.

Subheadings

Many scholarly works require only one level of subhead throughout the text. Some, particularly scientific or technical works, require more levels of subheadings. Sometimes editors have to add heads if a lengthy stretch of type does not contain one. Subheadings should be succinct, meaningful, and similar in tone.

When more than one level is used, the subheads should be set as A heads (the principle subhead), B heads (the secondary subhead), C heads, and so on.

Follow outline style. If using a secondary subheading, then provide at least one other secondary subheading under the same principal subheading. However, in cases when outline style seems contrived, it is acceptable to make an exception to this rule.

Example:
Principle Subhead
Secondary Subhead
Run-in Subhead.

Delete "The" or "A" when they are the first words of a subheading, if possible. Never include a reference citation in a subhead.

Capitalize the initial letter of the first and last words and all other words except articles, conjunctions, "to" in infinitives, and prepositions.

Tables

Separate tables from text and create a new Word document for each.

Ensure that all tables are numbered consecutively (beginning with Table 1) and that all tables are called out in text.

Ensure that data given in text match those displayed in tables. Text should explain, not simply repeat, data displayed in tables.

Authors must provide written permission from the original copyright holder if tables are adapted or are to be reprinted. Authors are responsible for any fees involved in obtaining permission for reprinting. Source lines for tables must contain complete publication information for the original table, including the page number. When the permission letter from the original copyright holder specifies language, that language should be reproduced exactly.

Column Heads

Edit column heads for sense and capitalization/lowercase style. Information given in parentheses in column heads should be lowercased (for example, "in months"). Symbols that apply to the entire column (for example, %, $) should be in parentheses in the heading only and not repeated in the body of the table.

Ideally, only one category of information should go under each column head. Sometimes it is necessary to add column heads. However, if the table will be too wide to fit the printed page with the addition of new column heads, new column heads can be added within the table body, or the units can be clearly indicated in the stub heads.

Stub Heads

Edit stub heads for sense and consistency and initial cap.

Body

Check math wherever possible and query author about discrepancies.
Insert commas after thousands (2,025 not 2025).
Edit for en and em dashes.
Text columns should be as succinct as possible. The first word in each entry should be capped; add a period at the end of complete sentences only. Entries in a column should be as parallel in structure as possible.

Notes

For ordering of notes and source lines, see Figures section.

Usage

Refer to the following pages for terms to avoid and terms to use. Consult *Webster's* (11th ed.) for terms not found on this list. Use only the primary spelling listed in *Webster's*.

and/or	Use one or the other; "or" is usually better. Otherwise, rephrase to read, "A, B, or both."
cf.	Means "compare" not "see."
due to	Do not use for "because of" in adverbial phrases. "Due," an adjective, should be attached only to a noun or pronoun.
e.g.	Use "for example."
employ	Use only in reference to working, otherwise use "use."
etc.	Use "and so on" or "and so forth."
execute	Use "implement."
feel	Use only for emotions, not as a substitute for "think" or "believe."
i.e.	Use "that is."
impact	Do not use impact as a verb. Use "have an impact" or "affect." Do not overuse impact as a noun; use "effect" when appropriate.
in order to	The word "to" is usually enough.
prior to	Use "before."
service	Do not use service as a verb. Use "serve" or "provide service to."
since	Use only when referring to time.

the fact that The word "that" is usually enough.

utilize   Use "use."

via   Use "through" or "by" unless referring to electronic transmissions, highways, or other routes of transportation.

where   Use only when referring to geographical location.

while   Use only when referring to time.

Acronyms

The following acronyms do not need to be spelled out on first mention:

AAIDD

AIDS

CD-ROM

DSM

GED

HIV

HMO

IQ

IV

PhD

SPSS

Also, parties and state affiliations of members of Congress are abbreviated in parentheses.

Example:

Barbara Mikulski (D-MD)

University Names

Variations occur in the way some universities (often within the same university system) refer to themselves. Preferred usage for some of these institutions is as follows:

Rutgers, The State University of New Jersey, New Brunswick

State University of New York (SUNY) at Buffalo

University at Albany, State University of New York

University at Buffalo, State University of New York

University of California, Berkeley

University of California, Los Angeles

University of California, San Diego

University of California, San Francisco

University College, University of Maryland, College Park

University of Maryland at Baltimore

University of Maryland, Baltimore County

University of Maryland, College Park

University of Minnesota, Bloomington

University of Minnesota-Minneapolis

University of North Carolina at Chapel Hill

University of Texas, Arlington

University of Texas at Austin

University of Wisconsin—Madison

University of Wisconsin—Milwaukee

Foreign Languages

Occasionally a manuscript contains words or text in a foreign language. If the word or phrase is in *Webster's*, then it is considered to have become part of the English language (so it is not italicized). Be sure to check that the spelling (including diacritics) is correct (if you cannot verify). If the word is not in *Webster's*, then italicize it and include or query for a parenthetical translation (if the meaning is not clear from the context).

Part III
Submission and Publication

Journal Submissions

This chapter is an overview of the process of submitting an article to a particular journal. It includes a general description of the entire process and specific instructions for submitting an article for review. The overview, although tailored for the journals at AAIDD, can be extended to other journals and even books.

Knowledge of the lifecycle of an article in the journal production process is helpful in two ways. First, it makes the process familiar so that there will be fewer miscommunications among author and editor, copyeditor, typesetter, and printer. Second, familiarity with the process allows the author to anticipate what materials might be requested at any point in the process. In general, the auxiliary materials sometimes overlooked are copyrights or permissions to reprint information and particular citations. In addition to peer review, copyright, permissions, and knowledge of what constitutes "fair use" or what is or is not considered to be in the public domain is covered in the following chapters. In some cases, the information is objective and clear; in other cases, the information is subjective and confusing. It is when the information is subjective that editors are of tremendous help.

Preparing to Submit

The manuscript being submitted for consideration must meet the basic requirements of (a) extending the literature and (b) the target audience has been properly identified. In conjunction with properly identifying the audience, there is a "goodness of fit" to consider in selecting which journal is the best for submission. For AAIDD, this means choosing between *American Journal on Intellectual and Developmental Disabilities* and *Intellectual and Developmental Disabilities*.

In brief,

> The *American Journal on Intellectual and Developmental Disabilities (AJIDD)* is the leader in reporting ground-breaking research in the biological, behavioral, and educational sciences. Since 1886, AJIDD has been an essential reference for institutions, libraries, professionals, and students seeking to stay up-to-date in the fields of biology, health sciences, human services, psychology, intellectual disabilities, and/or education. (AAIDD, n.d.)

Intellectual and Developmental Disabilities (IDD) is a practitioner's journal of practice, policy, and perspectives.

> IDD is dedicated to meeting the information needs of those who seek effective ways to help people with intellectual disability. The journal reports new teaching approaches, program developments, administrative tools, program evaluation, service utilization studies, community surveys, public policy issues, training and case studies, and current research in intellectual disability. (AAIDD, n.d.)

Choosing Where to Submit

Using the AAIDD journal descriptions as a guide will help direct the author to the best fit for a particular work. Depending on how cross-disciplinary the subject matter is, this choice may not be simple in other academic realms. The best first step is always to go to the journal's Internet presence, whether that is the journal page itself at the Association or the particular disciplinary section. As section field offices tend to move from institution to institution, the first place to look is the Association Web site (i.e., www.aaidd.org for AAIDD). The second place to look is the section for the journal. Finally, as happens more and more, the information for a journal might be at the commercial printer's Web portal.

If the journal has no Web presence, which is an increasingly unlikely scenario, information about the journal can usually be found on the inside cover of the journal itself. Most libraries at universities often maintain physical subscriptions, so if a number of article searches or citations seem to point to a particular journal, and that journal is either not online or is behind a pay wall, it is only a matter of getting to the library. Independent scholars should be able to get access to the physical copy as well without having to check it out of the library, and a cell phone makes an excellent photo copier. Typically associations, and AAIDD is no different in this respect, will usually sell single copies.

Reading the journal itself over the course of several volumes will, of course, provide the best experience in determining whether the article is an appropriate fit for the journal. Typically, one would want to be a subscriber to the journal or find that a subscription would be the best way to stay up-to-date in the field. Media have diversified over the last two decades, as online presence has allowed for less "gatekeeping" in getting materials published, and some academic pursuits are not appropriate for a journal but may be essential to an article (i.e., documentary film in anthropological ethnography). This has led to a renaissance in how ideas are being published and what is considered legitimate in the academic realm. Some materials are marked as raw data, some are sourced online, and some articles themselves are made available before publication with the caveat that it is not to be considered a "final" work. The level of legitimacy each association, editor-in-charge, and discipline chooses for each of these types of auxiliary materials is a strong factor to consider when submitting. For example, some science disciplines, such as neuro-psychology, need to be on an extremely short run for publication because the information published by one group may be essential to another group in the process of validating or challenging that work: assessment, replicability, and testing the conclusion.

How to Submit

To submit an article to one of AAIDD's journals, please go to the "Publications" tab at the main page of the Association Web site (www.aaidd.org). Information can be found in the "Author Center": book proposal guidelines, journal editorial policies, and journal submissions. For *American Journal on Intellectual and Developmental Disabilities* and *Intellectual and Developmental Disabilities*, Allen-Track™ powers the manuscript tracking system that initiates the submissions process. Under "Journal Submissions," each journal has a direct link to take the author to that Web portal. The author registers and uploads the article. Instructions follow, but, in general, an author can expect between 8 and 10 weeks to hear back on the initial review.

It is essential to bear in mind that all identifying information within the text of the submitted article should be changed for the sake of anonymity. That includes, but is not limited to, citations for one's own work, initials or names in dialogue, figure notes or notes in tables, endnotes, and specific locales (i.e., university affiliations) that might point to the author's identity. It is easy to overlook something, and counterproductive to be overzealous. For example, the entirety of a personal reference in the references cited can be deleted and replaced with "Author. (YYYY)," and reinserted later; however, removing one's own name from an edited volume that is the citation for another author will create a glaring omission that readily reveals one's identity. This is a "security thorough obscurity" strategy that does more to protect anonymity than to try to sanitize all possible references.

What to Expect

As noted, sometime around the 8 to 10-week mark, contact will be made by the appropriate editor-in-charge, and the initial revisions process will begin. Once accepted, the process transfers to the AAIDD Publications Department, and coordination will continue from there.

Journal Process

Articles follow a fairly typical path in academic journals. The entire process, called *production,* has between six and eight discernible steps, depending on the journal and the organization. These steps are, in short, as follows: (1) submission and acceptance, (2) peer review, (3) substantive edit, (4) copyedit, (5) proofs, (6) galleys, and (7) publication. For further information and a similar overview of this process, see *Chicago Manual of Style* (2010, ch. 2.2).

Submission and Acceptance

The particulars of how to submit an article will be covered later. Once an article has been submitted to a journal, the editor will read it and determine whether it is a good fit for the journal. Several factors affect this decision. It might be accepted outright. It might be considered publishable but would fit a particular theme issue down the road. In that case, it might thereby be accepted but not for publication in the typical life cycle of article production. It might be rejected but with specific revisions requested and an invitation to resubmit. Or it might be rejected outright. An article that has been rejected for revision and resubmission is actually a good sign and the path that most published articles take. Editors would not suggest improvements without having given it a thorough read and would not thoroughly read something that is not considered publishable by the journal.

Once an article has passed through initial submission or resubmission, it is considered accepted. Typically, the article will have been processed in a database either by the author or editor, and it will be ready to send out for review.

Peer Review

Peer review has different requirements for each discipline and generally occurs as part of the submission and acceptance process. The purpose of peer review is to independently determine the fit and veracity of the work within the context of the discipline and also the constraints of the journal, its style, and its audience. For a more comprehensive overview of peer review, please see the following chapter.

Substantive Edit

For AAIDD journals, the substantive copy edit is carried out by the editor-in-charge and the reviewers who weigh in with generally specific skills. The editor-in-charge and reviewers have done the majority of the work during the revise/resubmit process by directing the piece and challenging the science.

Copy Edit

Copyediting is a mechanical process that is much more black and white than the substantive edit, but that process is also often confusing and obscure. Whereas the editor-in-charge and the reviewers are expert in the science, discipline, terminology, and other literature of the field, the AAIDD staff editor is expert in the institutional knowledge, the style preferences, and the limitations of language. That is, whereas the editor-in-charge is concerned with the forest, the staff editor is concerned with the trees.

A copy edit encompasses manuscript preparation, reference cross-checks, ensuring all elements are included, a mechanical grammar edit (parallelism, dangling modifiers, mixed metaphors, acronyms defined, superfluous language, inconsistent terms, etc.), editing for house style, and spell checking. A staff editor who has spent much time with a journal or within a particular discipline has such specific knowledge of a particular journal that queries regarding substantive queries not addressed during the submission process might still arise.

Copyediting is about the "feel" of the article and how that fits in with the journal's presentation. Thus, the staff editor takes all the information on hand to that point and synthesizes it with several things in mind. He or she will check the structure of the article, argument cohesion, do some copyediting for clarity, and cut or ask for additional material according to page limits. This tends to be the time he or she will ensure that abstracts, key words, acknowledgments, and running heads are included. This stage is more about the presentation of the article than the science itself. After the staff editor has completed this stage will be the last time the author will see the manuscript before publication, as often queries arise regarding meaning, intent, references, and citations. One or two rounds between author and staff editor—who takes corrections from the author, integrates them into a "final" version, and sends it to the printer for layout and typesetting—might be required for the staff editor to be comfortable releasing it for publication.

Proofs

Once the final manuscript has been submitted to the typesetter by the staff editor, a "proof" is generated. The article is set to the page how it will likely look in printed form, usually with pagination. Proofing is the last chance for the staff editor to ensure that there are no typos, strange spaces, inconsistencies, lost text, or improperly spaced tables or figures. Pagination can still change because other articles are now with the complete issue. An article is not considered final yet, although very few changes are encouraged at this point.

Galleys

Galleys are the very last spot proof that staff editors perform to ensure an entire issue is ready to release to print. A number of modern printers have eliminated or conflated this stage with what used to be called *bluelines* (a print of the issue that was a negative plate of the pages as they would roll off press). The galley stage is now usually the final stage of the process in which any change can be made.

Publication

Once the article, along with the entire issue, is released to press, the printer makes copies, binds the issue, and mails it to subscribers. AAIDD provides courtesy copies of the print journals to each of the article authors.

References

American Association on Intellectual and Developmental Disabilities. (n.d.). Journals. http://aaidd.org/content_577.cfm?navID=154, accessed July 15, 2012

Chicago manual of style (16th ed.). (2010). Chicago: Author.

Peer Review

Peer review has different requirements for each discipline and most often occurs as part of the submission and acceptance process. This cycle is the result of an evolution of a process and not the application of tradition. That is, peer review has evolved over the years to serve a specific purpose: to improve the science while simultaneously preparing the finished work for publication. Because reviewers are usually selected from experts in the field discussed in the article, the process of peer review is considered critical to establishing a reliable body of research and knowledge. Scholars reading the published articles rely on the peer-review process to provide reliable and credible information that they can build on for subsequent or related research.

Various peer-review techniques are in common use. Anonymity may be unilateral or reciprocal (*single-blind* or *double-blind*). In single-blind reviewing, the reviewers know who the authors are, but the reviewers remain anonymous. Another approach is the double-blind review, wherein neither the reviewer nor the author knows the identity of the other. Double-blind peer review is perhaps the most reliable form of the process in the respect that it fosters unvarnished criticism and discourages favoritism or bias in publication decisions. However, despite the preference for double-blind review, it is often very difficult to achieve consistently in practice. Often, experienced reviewers can determine an author's identity on the basis of subject area, reference citations, and writing style.

Procedure

In the case of AAIDD publications, the editor-in-charge sends submitted manuscripts to researchers or scholars who are expert in the field through a Web-based manuscript tracking system (MTS). Usually, there are two or three reviewers assigned to any given manuscript.

The reviewers then evaluate the work, returning their feedback to the editor-in-charge via the MTS, with notes regarding the weaknesses, suggestions for improvement, and publication recommendations. Most suggestions are as follows: unconditional acceptance; acceptance pending specific improvements; invitation to revise and resubmit; or rejection outright. The editor-in-charge then analyzes the reviewers' comments and recommendations in conjunction with his or her own opinion of the manuscript before rendering a publication decision. The role of the reviewer is advisory, and the editor is under no obligation to accept the reviewers' opinions. Typically, the author will receive the reviewer feedback with the editor's decision letter.

AAIDD Policy

The following is an overview that can be found under the Editorial Policy page of the AAIDD Web site:

> Each submitted paper is reviewed by experts in the area of the paper's content. To be published, a paper must conform to the highest standards of professional development of the disciplines identified with its content. Research papers are judged on the importance of the questions asked, soundness of conceptualization and rationale, relevance of research operations to the questions, reliability of results, logic of conclusions, and clarity and economy of presentations. Reports of studies using educational and psychological tests designed for practical use are accepted only if the tests meet the criteria described in the *Standards for*

Educational and Psychological Testing (American Psychological Association, 1985). Literature reviews, theoretical reinterpretations, and scholarly reassessments are judged on relevance of focus, incisiveness with which issues are defined, completeness of coverage of relevant literature, consistency in the application of evaluative criteria, soundness of inferences and conclusions, and novelty and probable fruitfulness of interpretation. Such papers must include new insights in order to be acceptable for publication. [AAIDD, n.d.]

Peer review is a murky subject, and it is worth noting that few programs in academia prepare an author for exactly what the process entails. In the December 2012 issue of *American Anthropologist,* Editor-in-Chief Tom Boellstorff and an author from a previous issue take a direct look into the peer review process. The primary reviewer agreed to reveal her identity to help illuminate what one can expect from a reviewer; the three then dissect the conversations that take place among reviewer, editor, and author. Using passages from at least four versions of the draft that was eventually published as an article in the journal, they reveal the step-by-step process by which an article is shaped for publication once it has received final acceptance. This piece is a useful primer on peer review in action. It is noteworthy that anticipating the process through familiarization can ease the discomfort that rigorous review can cause. The main lesson to take from this is that the level of communication that occurs between principle agents is the key to successful and satisfactory review.

Later Changes

At the copyediting stage, which follows peer review, the focus shifts to polishing the manuscript for final print. At that point, any major changes to the argument, science, or the addition or dropping of data should be discouraged. There are, of course, cases in which something vital to the argument was cut or lost during review, and this will necessitate further review before the final version may be forwarded to production (see *Chicago Manual of Style*, 2010, sec. 2.5).

References

American Association on Intellectual and Developmental Disabilities. (n.d.). Editorial policy. http://aaiddjournals.org/page/policy/ajidd

Chicago manual of style (16th ed.) (2010). Chicago: Author.

Vora, Neha, & Boellstorff, Tom. (in press). Anatomy of an article: The peer review process as method. *American Anthropologist* 114(4).

Copyright and Permissions

This chapter is a compendium of the most common questions that arise regarding copyright and permissions during the publishing process. It is not meant to be exhaustive—just informative. As always, it is best to research what disciplinary expectations are regarding copyright and requesting permissions from an institution, in general, and a journal, in particular.

Copyright

What to Expect as the Author

In general, authors must transfer copyright to the publisher of a journal. This is to allow for the publisher to pursue the improper use of a published work. This protects the author's interests as well as those of the publishing entity. Because copyright laws for intellectual property holders in the United States are so stringent, it is far more difficult for an individual to pursue damages than it is for a publishing entity. Unlike for works of fiction, in which first-run rights are often granted and then transferred to the author, in nonfiction, and in particular for academic publishing, the transfer of copyright has become standard. In general, the stakes for scientific authorship can be greater than for those of fiction in that it is likely that more than one author or group could be working on the same subject matter in a way that would be considered not only unique (as with fiction) but also competitive (as with nonfiction).

Competing Versions

One of the issues that can arise in academic publishing is the possibility of a series of works that can be nearly identical. As specialists in a field, the publishing arc would necessarily tend to narrow or overlap for a group or author over time. As such, the primary concern with the transfer of copyright is to ensure that no competing versions exist. That is, if a conference paper has been converted to an article, each version must be identifiably different. The natural course of review tends to ensure that papers change en route to publication, sometimes significantly, and this concern eliminates itself. In the case of works that share an origin point, it is helpful to note that point in an acknowledgments section, even though the end result would be considered intellectually unique through copyright. In addition to delineating noncompeting copies of a work, the acknowledgments language should make it clear that individuals are being thanked for help during the process of review on drafts of the manuscript and not directly on the final product (which would require coauthorship credit) and that the draft is just that, only a draft (or "version" in more modern parlance).

However, some disciplines have similar journals, and submitting the same work to more than journal (often called *overlapping submissions*) is discouraged. Submitting a previously published article is certainly discouraged for copyright reasons, but not necessarily for permissions reasons. In using previously published material within a manuscript submission or in the entirety of a manuscript, copyright may not necessarily reside with the author, photographer, or even the journal in which the material was initially published. Because of publisher acquisitions and/or a journal itself going out of print, who owns the copyright can become a murky business, and, in essence, copyrights can be lost or "orphaned." It is the author's responsibility to discover the owner of the copyright and to obtain permission to use the material. It is not enough to get the permission of the author of a work, although, as a professional courtesy that is a good practice. Permissions will be double checked by a copyeditor and an accepted manuscript will be pulled from the publication slate if it is found to be wanting in that respect. This is the most common hang-up that can occur late in the publishing process and can become a massive headache for the unprepared author—especially if the copyright-protected material in the manuscript cannot be easily edited out without compromising the science or triggering further peer review.

Permissions

In academic publishing, the dissemination of information is and ought to be valued above the material interests of a publisher. Copyright should be defended for improper use of a work, as defined by established and evolving case law; but academic freedom is a tradition that predates all the laws to which a work is currently subject in the United States. As such, permissions tend to be freely given (although not necessarily given freely), depending on the context. Nominal fees are asked for the processing of requests, if the institution determines that permission can be granted.

Most institutional publishers announce boiler plate permissions instructions that appear to restrict the use in any way of its materials. An example of such can be found on the AAIDD Web site, which, at first blush, appears to contradict the spirit of academic freedom:

> AAIDD's printed, electronic, and audiovisual materials may not be republished, reprinted, or distributed without written permission or contractual agreement with AAIDD. (AAIDD, n.d.)

However, in the following paragraphs, the boundaries are extended to those areas dictated by discipline and case law. It is useful to be familiar with where the boundary resides between the permissions that an institution can demand and the requirements dictated by fair use (see chapter "Fair Use and Public Domain").

Permission Requests

Part of academic freedom is the right to disseminate information. As such, the contents of an article are not typically intended only for journal subscribers. For permission to use the material in another form (such as referring to data or an image in a new work), formal permission must be sought. AAIDD's Web site notes this as follows:

> AAIDD will grant permission to use copyrighted material from AAIDD journals, books, and audiovisual materials. Include in your written request for permission the publication title and the chapter or article title(s) that you are interested in; volume, issue, and page numbers; copyright year; the purpose of the requested use; number of photocopies you plan to make; the name and address of your publisher if you intend to publish. (n.d.)

Republishing

If a work is to be republished in another format, which is a special exemption to the competing versions ethos, the rightsholder has both the right of refusal and the right to request payment for the appearance of that work. Again, although copyright has transferred to the publisher, an institution can honor the rights of the author as the originator of a work.

> AAIDD frequently receives requests to republish articles from its journals in formal books. AAIDD generally will grant permission, contingent on agreement from the author and payment of a fee. If the author does not agree to having the article republished in a book, AAIDD will not grant permission. (AAIDD, n.d.)

Reprinting

For journal articles, formal permission to reprint is not typically required. This is primarily for ease in disseminating materials within the classroom or other academic environment. AAIDD's Web site makes explicit the dividing line between articles and books.

. . . contracts with copy houses permit copying without prior consent from journal articles only. Permissions for reprinting any portion of an AAIDD book must be requested on an individual basis. (n.d.)

A Note on NIH-Funded Research

If the work has received funding from the National Institutes of Health (NIH), the "right of the public" requires further rigors for transparency. As such,

. . . a "Public Access Policy" has been adopted by the National Institutes of Health pursuant to congressional mandate. This policy requires submission, for posting on the National Library of Medicine's PubMed Central, of the final manuscripts of all peer-reviewed articles derived from NIH-funded research. Manuscripts are to be submitted upon final acceptance for publication—that is, after the entire peer review and editorial process is complete and the article is ready for publication. [*Chicago Manual of Style*, 2010, sec. 4.64]

References

American Association on Intellectual and Developmental Disabilities. (n.d.). Copyrights and permissions. http://www.aaidd.org/content_7802.cfm?navID=370

Chicago manual of style (16th ed.) (2010). Chicago: Author.

Fair Use and Public Domain

Fair Use

As technology has grown, so have the tools of plagiarism. The standard for citing the work of others has not changed in the "cut-and-paste" era, but the ease with which information has become available has drastically changed. Technological leaps test the boundaries of traditional academic scholarship, and commercial practices often bleed over into the less materialistic arena of scholarship. Before the mimeograph, the copy machine, and electronic filing, the cost of reproduction was higher and more of a deterrent. Copyrights were easier to administer. Before the film industry, book copyrights were easier to administer. Now a crisscrossing of rights claimants, in several countries, can complicate what should be a straightforward process in citing the work of others.

The concept of "fair use" is an exception to copyright that is carved out in the interests of the commons. It allows for such things as making personal copies of copyrighted work that are not intended for commercial gain. The landmark U.S. Supreme Court case commonly called the "Betamax Case," 464 U.S. 417 (1984), for example, granted that it was not a violation of copyright to make a recording of a television show for the purpose of time shifting it (i.e., watching when it was most convenient, rather than only at the time of broadcast). This decision opened up an entire industry in the manufacture of video-recording devices and home video rentals, as it created a safe haven for them. In addition, it spawned new case law in determining the limits of other copying technologies that followed in its wake, namely file sharing over networks.

The effects of this decision overlap in the arena of academic publishing only insofar as the dissemination of information is concerned. There are four components used in determining fair use.

Purpose and Character

The "purpose and character" relates to its most basic identifying feature. Is it a commercial work, or is it work in the public domain? Is it intended for a paying audience, subscription, or freely available?

Nature of Work

The nature of work is the necessary qualities used in determining how the work may be used. That is, is it fiction, is it data, is it a movie? If a movie, is it documentary or commercial, harking back to the "purpose and character" clause? In short, how is it bound to copyright?

Amount and Substantiality

The "amount and sustainability" provision of fair use regards the amount of information being cited in consideration of the two above provisions. This provision covers how much of a copyrighted work may be used without then violating the terms of the copyright. In academic publishing, an institution will likely explicitly note to what extent it regards the fair use of its works and will require permission to be granted for anything further (see "What an Author May Use" section of this chapter).

Effect of Use

Finally, the "effect of use" provision in the exceptions granted by fair use covers the potential damage that might be caused by citing the information. If one cites the entirety of a poem, even if it is less than the length typically allowed by publishers (i.e., 300 congruent words requiring citation), it might be considered damaging to the copyright holder. The publishing entity might either make it more readily available without granting the fees to which the rights holder is entitled or make commercial gain thereby without due compensation.

What an Author May Use

In determining what AAIDD grants in the fair use of its own published works, see the Association Web site where the following language is posted:

> Fair Use: In accordance with industry standards, authors may use excerpts from AAIDD books of up to 300 words, except for figures or tables, without requesting formal permission or paying fees. Full attribution is expected. Tables and figures may not be reprinted without written permission. . . .
>
> In accordance with the Fair Use Section of the Copyright Act of 1976, AAIDD will grant permission to photocopy articles or abstracts from AAIDD journals for one-time use for the purpose of research, scholarship, training, professional development, and education without payment of a fee. This provision includes one-time use of multiple copies in classrooms, agencies, or for distribution at a seminar. (AAIDD, n.d.)

Public Domain

In the United States, in general, a work remains under copyright for 75 years after the author's death. There are certain exceptions to this rule, depending on whether the work was published and the timing of the death of the author would make what would ordinarily be an orphaned work subject to copyright. In addition, international publishing agreements complicate what is already a complicated matter regarding works subject to copyright.

Fortunately, the vast majority of works cited for academic publication fall under the fair use provision, and citing the work comes down to a few simple rules.

Citing Public Domain Works

Works clearly in the public domain, such as those by Shakespeare, require the minimum amount of information necessary to find the quote being used. The author's name and work in text, with a year of publication optional (if known).

Citing Orphaned Works

Orphaned works are works in which the copyright holder cannot be found or identified but that if the holder were known that work would fall under the normal rules of copyright. A typical case would be works found within a publication no longer extant. The publication no longer has a claimant for copyright, but the authors may or may not claim copyright for individual pieces, depending on the original signed agreement. Such agreements are usually difficult to find, and authors have a choice about how to proceed. Two authors within the same publication may make different copyright claims, especially if the work is fiction. In the case of orphaned works, best practices dictate that the work be cited as if the copyright holder were known and the copyright active.

Derivative Works

Derivative works are those works that are based in some way on a public domain source but are themselves subject to copyright. The classic example in academic publishing is translated work. The works of Plato may be in the public domain, but English translations of the work are subject to copyright if they meet the standards set forth by law (i.e., the translator is not deceased or has not been deceased for longer than 75 years). If the translation has been made from the source by a submitting author, it is not considered derivative in terms of citing and so requires only the minimal citation information noted in "Citing Public Domain Works."

Derivative works are to be cited according to the normal citation convention of the publishing entity. Often, this is the author–date convention for in-text citation and full publication information in a References section.

Final Note

When in doubt as to how far fair use extends, whether a work is orphaned, or whether it is subject to copyright or in the public domain, it is better to treat the source as if it is and to fully cite and reference the information. Editors-in-chief and copyeditors are well-versed in the rules for citation and may either (a) ask whether the author wishes to strike extraneous information or (b) query for full citation information.

References

American Association on Intellectual and Developmental Disabilities. (n.d.). Copyrights and permissions. http://www.aaidd.org/content_7802. cfm?navID=370

Index

CPSIA information can be obtained at www.ICGtesting.com
Printed in the USA
BVOW042002170912

300524BV00005BA/1/P

9 781937 604080